The Art of Play

*an interactive program designed to
encourage enthusiasm for the Integrated Arts
in preschool-age children*

The Art of Play

*an interactive program designed to
encourage enthusiasm for the Integrated Arts
in preschool-age children*

Laura L. Wagner

Originator of the Creative Arts Program (CAP)

The Art of Play
an interactive program designed to encourage enthusiasm for
the Integrated Arts in preschool-age children
© 2011
By Laura L. Wagner

ISBN-13: 978-1-4681135-1-8

Cover and Interior Design – Holly Rosborough,
Network Printing Services
Editor – Gina Mazza

Wagner Publishing
Allison Park, PA 15101

10 9 8 7 6 5 4 3 2 1

What Educators Are Saying about the Creative Arts Program (CAP) and *The Art of Play* Curriculum

Being exposed to the arts helps children become well rounded.
– Tracy Connolly

Children are learning the beauty of spoken language and storytelling. They are experiencing the human element of entertainment that is missing in television and movies.
– Marilyn Limbacher

CAP allows young students to think outside the box.
– Michelle Kerber

We love sign language and we use it a lot in our classroom.
– Carol O'Malley

Learning about the arts builds self-esteem, fosters interest and participation in the creative arts beyond our doors.
– Tammy Simon

We love the CAP curriculum! I feel that this has opened up the children's eyes to new things, new experiences and new ways of thinking.
– Kate Miller

I was surprised when even the very quiet and shy children in my class got up and participated. It's active learning at its best.
– Judy Hummel

We enjoyed the talents of Laura Wagner's character of Miss Floretta.
– Kitty Irlbacher

Table of Contents

An Introduction to CAP

The Creative Arts Program (CAP) is an integrative arts program that provides children with a broad exposure to fine arts through the age-appropriate use of dramatic play and interactive storytelling. Each session is approximately 30 minutes in length and focuses on an entertaining story with a central artistic theme.

The program targets multiple intelligences (Howard Gardner, 1983) so that children, depending on how they process information, have the opportunity to learn through seeing, hearing, touch and experience. Areas of emphasis include American Sign Language (ASL), puppets, costumes, lighting, sound effects, movement, creative writing, music, visual art, public speaking, performance, masks, theatre etiquette and more.

Laura Wagner, the originator of CAP, received her Bachelor of Arts in Theatre Education and a Master in Fine Arts from the University of Montana. The character of Miss Floretta, whom you will meet on the following pages, is the brainchild of Ms. Wagner. As Miss Floretta, Ms. Wagner facilitates each CAP session and entertains the students in a way that makes learning fun and captivating.

Ms. Wagner is an accomplished performer, storyteller, teacher and Scottish bagpiper. She lives with her husband and son in Pittsburgh, Pennsylvania.

A Letter from Miss Floretta

It is good to be here together!

Hi Everyone! I am Miss Floretta and I want to thank you for joining me on an exciting adventure through the wonderful world of Creative Arts! When you see my picture you will know that it is me talking to you and adding a personal thought to the lesson plan. Together we can create a vibrant, imaginative and safe environment in which our children can flower and grow.

Now get ready and get set... let's put our creative thinking "CAPs" on and see what limitless possibilities are inside. Enjoy!

Piggly Wiggly Puppets

 **AIM:** The purpose of this lesson is to introduce theatre etiquette, teach sign language, engage children's range of movement, spark creative physicalization and vocalization of a character and, finally, to utilize all of these new skills in the presentation of a story involving puppetry.

INTRODUCTION ACTIVITY:

Meet the Characters: Pick Animals from a Hat

Have the children sit or stand in a circle. Instruct each child to select an animal flash card from a hat and tell the class which animal they picked. Ask the child to make the sounds and movements of that animal. Each child joins in, continuing to choose animal cards as time allows. The teacher may need to lead sound and movement.

SECONDARY ACTIVITY:

Storytelling: *The Three Little Pigs* (Lang, 1895)

Have all students sit facing a "stage area" that is preset with three houses and an 'X' for the wolf. The story will be told twice, with the teacher first telling the story using pig puppets.

THROUGH ACTIVITY:

Put on a Show

Now it's the students' turn! The teacher will choose three students to be each pig and one student to be the wolf through an "audition." To do so, have all the children make their best "pig noise" on the count of three; proceed the same way when auditioning the part of the wolf.

Retell the story (perhaps with a little help from kids in the audience) of *The Three Little Pigs* having each student act out their part using pantomime and puppets. When it is time for the pigs to speak their lines, have the child use the puppet.

As the story continues, the child playing the wolf (who may be given a costume piece, if desired, such as a cape or top hat) acts out the part of the wolf. When the story is complete, have students take a bow. Prompt children in the audience to clap for the actors on stage. If time allows, recast the show and repeat.

BEYOND ACTIVITY:

Word play: *Five Pudgy Pigs* by Laura Wagner

Make sure the children pay careful attention to speaking slowly and with clear diction. Have them recite the following:

> *Five pudgy pigs*
> *went waddling by.*
> *One marched into the muck*
> *to eat a big mud pie!*
> **(repeat)**
> *Four pudgy pigs . . . three, two, one.*

SUPPLIES NEEDED:

Top hat filled with animal cards
Three pig puppets
Wolf costume (optional)
Familiarity with *The Three Little Pigs* story
Masking tape to mark the set on the floor

ASL: *(for reference, see www.aslpro.com)*

pigs, wolf, house, straw, sticks, bricks, scared, hungry, boiling water

This program is designed to cover multiple facets of the theatre. During this program, the kids are learning the following skills.

Theatre etiquette
Listening skills
Creativity
Puppetry
Sign language (ASL)
Performance skills
Memorization
Movement and speech
The joy of performing

Stage/audience formation
Spacial relations
Story structure
Body/mind connections
Character development
Public speaking skills
Self-esteem
Stage orientation

STAGE SET FOR THE "THREE LITTLE PIGS"

1st Pig's House

2nd Pig's House

3rd Pig's House

| 1 | 2 | 3 |

Wolf Stands Here

X

Stage

AUDIENCE

The three pigs are standing in their houses anxiously awaiting the big bad wolf!

The cast takes a bow.

Halloween Hullabaloo

 **AIM: The purpose of this lesson is to introduce basic mask work, prepare children for what it feels like to dress up as a character, nurture a child's affinity for costumes, and expose children to the art of creative writing by using their imaginations.**

INTRODUCTION ACTIVITY:

Character Work: What Are You Going to Be?

Have children stand in a circle and, one by one, tell the group what they are going to be for Halloween. Based on their responses, have the kids do a motion that prepares them for what this character does with their body and voice that may be different from what they do every day.

For example, if a child says "Batman," have all the kids flap their arms and pretend to fly. If a child says "ballerina," have the class twirl around and dance in place. Each mini-demonstration should only last two or three seconds. This simple activity exposes children to the fundamental idea of what it means to "be a character." It gives each child a chance to be in the spotlight and get excited about dressing up in a costume.

SECONDARY ACTIVITY:

Mask Work

A great way to transition to this portion of the lesson is to instruct the children how to sign "Happy Halloween." Since the ASL sign looks like you are putting on a mask, ask the children what the sign reminds them of then proceed to tell them that they will get to put on a real mask.

Have enough half-masks available for each member of the class (preferably animal masks that only cover the top portion of the face; these are available from a company called Oriental Trading). Distribute one mask per child. Children must be instructed that the mask they get is the mask they must wear, unless another child is mutually willing to swap.

Help the children put on their masks and make sure they are able to see and breathe adequately. Set up mirrors around the room in advance. Allow the children to take turns standing in front of the mirrors so they can observe themselves with the masks on. Instruct them to physically move their bodies as that animal or character would and to watch themselves in the mirror. Add sound effects. If time allows, take off all masks, put them back in the hat and distribute a different mask and repeat the process. Collect the masks when finished.

THROUGH ACTIVITY:

Creative Writing/Put on a Show

Together, you and the students will create your own adventure. Using the provided story, read aloud with the children. Ask them to be creative writers and help fill in the blanks. (Use the animals from the animal masks as guides so they know which animals to choose.)

Once the story is complete and given a title, audition the kids to cast the show. If the characters are a pig, cow and bear, for example, have the students make the best pig, cow and bear noises to choose the characters. Pre-mark the stage with tape in the provided design to create a set for your play.

Present the story by narrating and facilitating all of the movements on stage. The children will follow your lead. Once the story is finished, have your actors take a bow while the kids in the audience applaud. This exercise presents a good opportunity to teach good audience and stage etiquette.

SUPPLIES NEEDED:

Animal masks	Tape (to mark the stage)
Hat	Copy of story
Mirrors	Pen

ASL: *(for reference, see www.aslpro.com)*

Happy Halloween!

MISS FLORETTA SAYS...

It is surprising to observe that many children don't know what to do when they get into a costume. The introductory activity gives them a chance to practice what they will be for Halloween, all while attaching movement to an idea. Now they will know what to do with their bodies and voices when they put on the real costume and pretend to be a character.

Children love to wear masks and see what they look like in the mirror. Having masks of familiar animals not only allows them to use knowledge they already have (and are proud of) but also engage their bodies by using movement and sound. This quick exercise prepares them for the upcoming show that they will stage.

Creative writing is something that is not typically associated with preschoolers, but the fact that they do not write yet doesn't need to be a hindrance. In the tradition of *Mad Libs,* I have written a story template in which students can easily help fill in the blanks. In this way, they can actually help write the story that they will be presenting.

At this point in the program, the kids will have all the knowledge they need to participate and help create the story. Once it is written and titled, audition them using the same process as *The Three Little Pigs* exercise. Have the kids make the best animal noise they can and choose accordingly.

Once the show is cast, help to facilitate the action by having the audience help tell the story. This way, everyone is involved and engaged. When the actors take their bows at the end, it is always affirming to see their proud smiles.

Choosing characters and writing the story together.

Creative Writing Story Template

by Laura Wagner

TITLE: _____

Once upon a time there was a(n) _____(choose animal) that liked to go on many adventures with his/her best friend, the _____ (choose animal).

One day they were on a daring quest for the lost treasure of _____ (pick a treasure) that was hidden inside a tall _____(what?). To get to the treasure, they had to cross a big river filled with _____(could be anything!).

Off in the distance they spied the tall _____ and raced to the base only to meet a huge_____ (choose animal) standing guard. The friends were scared but they decided to demand the treasure, but the guard shook its head "no" and refused.

The friends then decided to tickle the guard but still it did not let them pass. The friends had to think really hard. Finally, they decided to offer a share of the treasure and the guard agreed!

They split the _____(treasure), traveled back across the river filled with _____, through the woods to their home. Once there, they were greeted like heroes (audience cheers)!

And they all lived happily ever after!

The End

STAGE SET FOR
CREATIVE WRITING PLAY

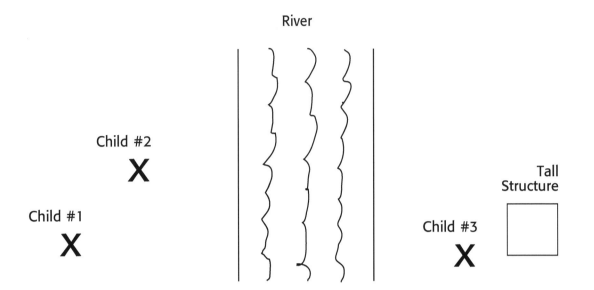

River

Child #2
X

Child #1
X

Tall
Structure

Child #3
X

AUDIENCE

Acting out our story.

Deciding how everyone will get the treasure.

Fruity Fun with Healthy Foods
(Version 1)

AIM: The purpose of this lesson is to expose children to a different cultural art form, cognitively discern what is and what is not a healthy food, reinforce how eating healthy food helps bodies grow big and strong, and how the food we eat affects how we physically feel.

INTRODUCTION ACTIVITY:

Healthy Food From a Hat

Inside your magic hat, place flash cards depicting different types of food; for example: apples, French fries or cake. Have each child pull a food from the hat and determine if the food is healthy by signing the word "yes" or "no." All children can join in on signing "yes" or "no." Go around in a circle until each child has had a turn to pull a food from the hat and decide whether or not it is healthy.

SECONDARY ACTIVITY:

Kamishibai Storycards (Japan) and
Momotaro: The Peach Boy by Miyoko Matsutani

Have the students sit in audience formation, ensuring that each can see the story cards. The instructor will deliver the story of *Momotaro: The Peach Boy* while sitting in a chair facing the children. After the story is completed, discuss how Momotaro ate nutritious foods and grew big and strong.

THROUGH ACTIVITY:

Stretch and Sing

Peaches and Apricots Stretch

Have children stand in a circle and repeat the word "peaches" while imagining that their bodies are becoming as small as they can be and their voices as high as they can make them. Next, say the word "apricots" as slowly as possible while stretching. Repeat several times in succession.

Apples and Bananas (Source: www.kididdles.com)

Continue standing in a circle. Sing the song "I Like to Eat Apples and Bananas." Create a poster sign with all the vowels printed out for the children to see while they are singing.

> *I like to eat, eat, eat, apples and bananas (repeat 2 times)*
> *I like to eat, eat, eat, epples and benenes (2 times)*
> *I like to oat, oat, oat, opples and bononos (2 times)*
> *I like to ite, ite, ite, ipples and bininis (2 times)*
> *I like to ute, ute, ute, upples and bununus (2 times)*
> *I like to ate, ate, ate, apples and bananas (2 times)*

SUPPLIES NEEDED:

Food flash cards
Kamishibai Storycards (visit www.Kamishibai.com)
Pre-made vowels poster

ASL: *(for reference, see www.aslpro.com)*

food, healthy, yes, no

Food Art: It's Okay to Play with your Food!
(Version 2)

AIM: The purpose of this lesson is to expose children to a new cultural art form, cognitively discern what is and what is not a healthy food, reinforce how eating healthy food helps our bodies grow big and strong, how the food we eat affects how we feel physically, and that food can be a source of inspiration for some artists.

INTRODUCTION ACTIVITY:

Healthy Food from a Hat

Inside your magic hat, place flash cards depicting different types of food—for example: apples, French fries or cake. Have each child pull a food from the hat and determine if the food is healthy by signing the word "yes" or "no." All children can join in on signing "yes" or "no." Go around in a circle until each child has had a turn to pull a food from the hat and decide whether or not it is healthy.

SECONDARY ACTIVITY:

Kamishibai Storycards (Japan) and
Momotaro: The Peach Boy by Miyoko Matsutani

Have the students sit in audience formation, ensuring that each can see the story cards. The instructor will deliver the story of *Momotaro: The Peach Boy* while sitting in a chair facing the children. After the story is completed, discuss how Momotaro ate nutritious foods, got plenty of rest and grew big and strong.

THROUGH ACTIVITY:

Food Art Slideshow

Have the students remain seated while they watch a slideshow projecting different images of food art—for example, a dog made from a banana, sheep made from cauliflower and olives, etc. Challenge the children to figure out which food is used in each picture. Explain that artists can find a way to create art with anything—even food!

BEYOND ACTIVITY:

Sing "Aiken Drum," a traditional Scottish song
(Source: www.kididdles.com)

Sing *a cappella* and clap with rhythm or sing with guitar. You can also draw the picture while you are singing to create a portrait of your character.

> *There was a man who lived on the moon, lived on the moon, lived on the moon.*
>
> *There was a man who lived on the moon and his name was Aiken Drum.*
>
> ***(Have children fill in the blanks with examples of healthy food)***
>
> *His hair was made from _____ (spaghetti, rice, string beans, etc.) (repeat word 3 times) and his name was Aiken Drum.*
>
> *His eyes were made from _____(blueberries, corn, apples, etc.) (repeat word 3 times) and his name was Aiken Drum.*
>
> ***(Continue with nose, mouth, ears, arms, legs, belly button and feet until all the kids have had a chance to contribute. Finish the song with first verse.)***

SUPPLIES NEEDED:

Food flash cards
Kamishibai Storycards (visit www.Kamishibai.com)
Prepared slideshow with food art
Computer/projector

Examples of food art for Food Art Slideshow: Google "food art images" or check out the book *Play With Your Food* by Joost Elffers

food, healthy, yes, no

MISS FLORETTA SAYS... (FOR BOTH VERSIONS 1 AND 2)

This lesson is effective in its simplicity. Exposure to healthy eating habits is vital to pre-school-aged children; this is the age when they are setting trends for a lifetime. This program teaches kids about nutrition in an artistic way.

Kamishibai Storycards are an amazing tool to educate and entertain children. *Kamishibai* is a storytelling tradition from Japan and the story cards absolutely fascinate children. Every child's eyes are glued to the cards. This is a story form that children most likely have never seen before; therefore, they are mesmerized from start to finish.

While some may argue that these lessons are somewhat sedentary for the topic of nutrition, the fact is that the students are engaged and actively learning at every moment. Kamishibai combined with the other activities creates a captive audience that is rarely seen in children this young. This lesson is not as "presentational" and "grand" as some of the others, but it creatively presents a simple message that the kids can grasp.

Finishing the lesson with a song ensures that the information is reaching different types of intelligences: musical, visual and kinesthetic *(Frames of Mind,* Howard Gardner, 1983). The children walk away with a new artistic enthusiasm, a deeper understanding of healthy choices, exposure to a new art form and a sense of wonderment that art can be discovered anywhere, even on a dinner plate.

NOTES

_____

_____

_____

_____

_____

_____

_____

_____

_____

_____

_____

_____

_____

_____

_____

_____

_____

_____

_____

_____

_____

_____

_____

_____

_____

_____

_____

_____

_____

Pow-Wow POW!
Native American Culture and the First Thanksgiving

AIM: The purpose of this activity is to expose children to the Native American culture in a respectful and authentic way, and introduce basic rhythm patterns in music, drumming, counting and poetry. It also familiarizes children with the history of the first Thanksgiving story.

INTRODUCTION ACTIVITY:

Welcome to my Pow-Wow!

Have Native American music playing as children enter the room. Have them sit in a circle around a "campfire", around which are various Native American objects such as a drum, buffalo fur, deerskin, talking stick, buffalo pictures and a Native American medicine bag. Also include a black hat in the display of items.

After an opening greeting, talk about what holiday is approaching and how Native Americans played a role in its origin. Discuss that a pow-wow is a gathering where music, storytelling, dancing and shared company takes place; also note to the students that you will be talking about rhythm. The first activity is basically talking about the holiday then passing around the artifacts so each student can experience the different textures, shapes and smells.

SECONDARY ACTIVITY:

Poetry Reading of *The First Thanksgiving,* and discussions on gratitude and the use of a talking stick

After each child gets a chance to hold each item, ask them which item looks like it does not belong with the others. Hopefully, at least one student will observe that the black hat does not belong. The teacher will then look inside the hat and discover a story inside; however, the story is out of order!

Use story cards numbered one through 10 to help the children put the story back in order. Explain that the story is a poem, which is just like a story but has rhythm to it. Read *The First Thanksgiving Story: Poem Style* (Source: www.tooter4kids.com) and emphasize the rhythm while you read. After the poem has been recited, highlight the main concepts of the story—for example, how the Pilgrims were very grateful for the food that the Native Americans helped them to grow. Give the students a few minutes to contemplate what they are grateful for in their lives.

Pick up the talking stick and explain that each student will get a turn to stand up, hold the stick and tell the group what they are grateful for and why (or if they can't think of anything, they can tell a story). Pass the talking stick around until everyone gets a turn.

THROUGH ACTIVITY:

Drumming and Rhythm

Now pick up the drum. Play a rhythm and see if the students can repeat it by patting the floor. Play several rhythms until the concept is grasped. (You may need to play the same rhythm over and over again.)

Next, have the students stand in a circle while the instructor plays a "walking beat"—or, a rhythm that matches the beat of walking. In return, everyone is to walk on the beat while going around in a circle. Once they get the hang of this, change the beat to double-time and ask them to match the new rhythm with their feet. After going around in a circle a few times, have them sit back down.

BEYOND ACTIVITY:

The Rain Game

If time allows, play *The Rain Game* (Source: www.teacherlink.edu). This gives the children an opportunity to use their bodies' natural four percussions: snapping, clapping, patting and stomping. Follow the rules of the game and explain how each sound really sounds like a rain storm. The children will love this! Close the exercise by thanking the children for joining in the pow-wow.

The Rain Game:

This game signifies a rainstorm starting soft, getting louder and louder until it is pouring with lightning and thunder, then the calm after the storm when it is quiet again. It is played with the teacher leading the students around a circle with the following actions:

- Silently rub your fingers together and ask students do the same.
- Rub your two hands together, making a very soft sound, and ask students to do the same.
- Very softly clap your hands together while the students follow (it should still be quiet).
- Snap your fingers.
- Go back to clapping and clap a little louder than you were snapping, then a little louder.
- Now clap loudly.
- Stomp your feet and clap, making a lot of noise.
- Now do it in reverse until there is silence again.

SUPPLIES NEEDED:

CD player	Deerskin
Native American music	Talking stick
Campfire	Drum
Buffalo picture	Numbered story cards
Buffalo fur	Black hat

ASL: *(for reference, see www.aslpro.com)*

Happy Thanksgiving, drum, thank you

Taking turns holding the talking stick and sharing what we are grateful for.

MISS FLORETTA SAYS...

The goal here is not only to establish an early appreciation for the arts but to expose children to different cultures, as well. Having been a student in the American West for a number of years, I've gained an understanding of the absolute importance of teaching Native American culture in a deeply respectful way. This lesson is my attempt to do just that.

Most of us are familiar with *The First Thanksgiving Story,* in which the Native Americans teach the Pilgrims how to plant crops; at harvest time, they share a big meal together and give thanks for their great abundance. Teaching this "traditionally accepted" version of the story is in accordance with school curriculum, so I decided to take this interpretation of the story and spin it in high favor of the Native Americans by teaching through the arts. Rhythm, drumming, rhythm in poetry, storytelling and listening to Native American music is an effective way to reach the children and teach pow-wow culture simultaneously.

I sincerely wanted this program to be as authentic and respectful as possible, so I contacted Kim Kapalka, a librarian at a Native American Museum. She was a tremendous asset to this lesson. She sent me authentic Native American paraphernalia to show my students: a piece of real bison fur, a talking stick, Native American art and a piece of bison hide. They got to experience Native American culture through hearing, seeing, smelling, doing and touching!

All the items placed in the center of our pow-wow.

Walking in Native Shoes

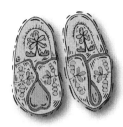 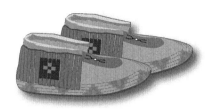 

 **AIM:** The purpose of this lesson is to introduce children to Native American culture, storytelling and the function of different types of shoes used to create a theatrical character.

INTRODUCTION ACTIVITY:

Whose Shoes?

Teach the students signs for the words "socks" and "shoes" and explain that they will be learning about shoes in this lesson. Pull from your hat several photographs of people wearing various types of shoes—for example, a doctor, cowboy, dancer and Native American—but don't show them to the kids yet!

With a different piece of paper, cover each photo revealing only the character's shoes. Show these to the children and see if they can guess who wears which type of shoe. Make sure the Native American photo is last so you can segue into the next topic of introducing them to Native American culture.

SECONDARY ACTIVITY:

Imagination Time: Try Them On!

Have all the children stand one side of the room and ask them to walk across the floor with their own shoes. Ask them how it feels to walk "in their own shoes." Instruct them to pretend that they are shaking off their real shoes and are going to try on the different types that are in the pictures.

Next, have the children pretend they are cowboys and cowgirls. Have them pretend to pull on cowboy boots and have them walk to the other side of the room as this character. Ask them to "kick off" their boots and try slipping on a comfortable pair of doctor's shoes.

To get them in character, tell them that they are in a hurry to get to their next patient, so have them walk at a quick pace in their supportive doctor shoes to the other side of the room.

Next, ask them to slip on dancing shoes and groove their way back across the floor.

Finally, have them slip on deerskin moccasins and walk very slowly and quietly, as if they are sneaking up on an animal in the woods. To close, have them walk quietly to the other side of the room then tiptoe their way to a seated circle.

THROUGH ACTIVITY:

Storytelling: *The Legend of the Snake with the Big Feet*

Have the children sit as they watch a presentation of this Native American legend.

BEYOND ACTIVITY:

Song: "I Have Two Shoes, How About You?"

Sing *a cappella* or with a guitar to the tune of "Skip to My Lou" (Source: www.kididdles.com).

> *I have two shoes, how about you?*
> *I have two shoes, how about you?*
> *I have two shoes, how about you?*
> *Stomp with your shoes like I do. (Stomp for 8 beats)*
>
> **(Repeat melody)**
>
> *I have two shoes, how about you? (3 times)*
> *Kick with your shoes like I do. (Kick for 8 beats)*

Continue to sing as the children offer their ideas for the last line and 8 counts of the song (kick, dance, fly, tiptoe, skip, tap, etc.).

SUPPLIES NEEDED:

Pictures of people with shoes (doctor, cow, dancer, native American)
Knowledge of the story
Knowledge of the song
Stuffed snake or puppet (optional)
Guitar (optional)

socks and shoes

MISS FLORETTA SAYS...

At preschool age, children are not often exposed to the idea that different jobs have different shoes, and that different shoes can affect the way you walk. This is a new and fascinating thought for them, and they loved pretending to try on different shoes and walk around in character. This is truly the beginning of theatrical character study as it is known!

It is also important for children this age to be exposed to different types of stories. Since storytelling is a rich Native American tradition, it's both fun and appropriate that the students hear an authentic Native American legend. The song at the end gives the children one more opportunity to use their bodies and imaginations before they go back to class.

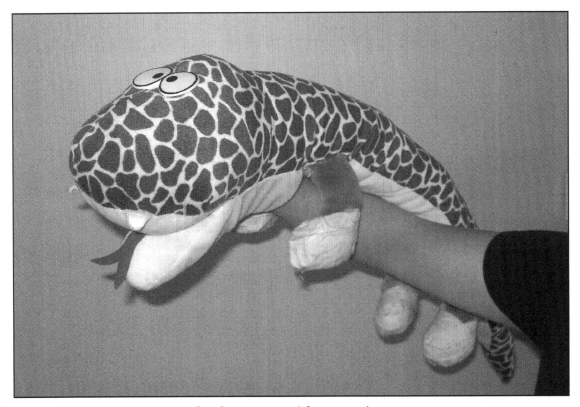

Snake puppet with moccasins.

The Legend of the Snake with Big Feet
A Native American Story

This traditional legend from an unknown author and tribe has been readapted for preschool children by Laura Wagner (original source: www.firstpeople.us).

Long ago, in the beginning of the world when only animals and Indians walked the land now called North America, a snake was born that was not like any other snake. Along his body were two sets of snake feet, complete with heels, arches and toes. The snake trotted along on these feet while the rest of its kind slithered along the ground. The other snakes scoffed at the young snake, saying that that far away from there lived other creatures with feet and that the footed snake should go live with them.

The poor snake had no choice but to leave his home, where he was not wanted. He traveled for a long time. The seasons changed, days became shorter and nights became longer. After many days of travel, the snake found a tribe of animals with feet. These creatures were not snakes; however, their skin was soft and smooth, and they stood tall and proud on their two feet.

The snake introduced himself to the tribe elders in their longhouse. [A long-house is a long, wooden house that is big enough to accommodate several families at one time.] "I know I have very little to offer you but I am a hard worker and a loyal soul. I can show your people how to protect their feet with deerskin covers. I call them moccasins."

The elders welcomed the little snake and the entire tribe treated it with kindness and equality. The snake joined them in all of their work, celebrations and traditions. It even sat at the chief's table during feasts. The chief, who loved the snake most of all, had a daughter who also thought the world of the snake. She would spend evenings listening to the snake's stories and they became great friends.

One day, while she was walking in the woods looking for porcupine quills to sew new moccasins, she found the little snake crying. She tried to comfort it, but the snake said that it had fallen in love with her. That made the snake sad because he knew she could never marry a snake.

She knew that this was true and it made her sad, too. Even though her father was a powerful chief, she never asked the forces of nature for anything before. But that night, she climbed the tallest hill and summoned the spirit of the sun with her voice and her magical drum.

"Oh, Sun Spirit! This good and kind snake has enriched our lives in many ways. Surely there is something you can do to help him!"

The Sun Spirit replied, "Go home to your lodge, build a fire. Play the music of your people and lay the snake in the center of the smoke."

The chief's daughter did as she was told. Out of the smoke walked a handsome young man. He stood tall and proud on his two feet, which were still covered with deerskin moccasins.

The snake, now a young man, had gotten his wish. The tribe members cheered! He went on to marry the chief's daughter and raise a generous and distinguished family. The elders say that this family became the *Pe jsik na tape,* or Snake Tribe of Indians.

The End

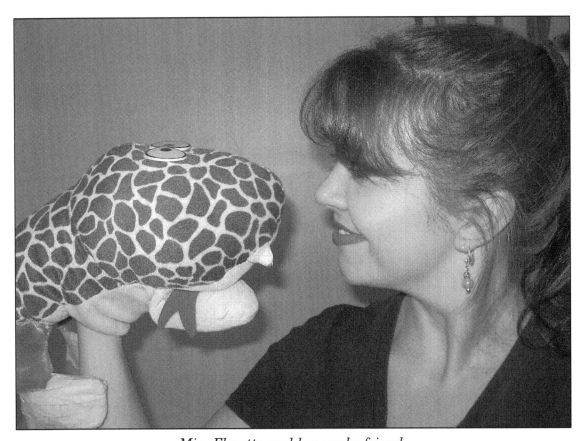

Miss Floretta and her snake friend.

NOTES

_____
_____
_____
_____
_____
_____
_____
_____
_____
_____
_____
_____
_____
_____
_____
_____
_____
_____
_____
_____
_____
_____
_____
_____
_____
_____
_____
_____
_____
_____

Christmas Puppet Dance

 **AIM:** The purpose of this lesson is to engage active listening skills, introduce the art of puppetry by manipulating and bringing a puppet to life, and introduce basic dance concepts.

INTRODUCTION ACTIVITY:

The Night Before Christmas by Clement C. Moore

Have students sit in audience formation or semi-circle in front of a home-made fireplace. Teach signs for "Santa," "reindeer" and "Merry Christmas" and ask children to watch for those words during the story.

Theatrically present the story using pantomime and ASL. During the telling of the story, set out boxes that look like wrapped presents. Inside each box should be ample sock puppets for each child in class (to be used in the next section).

SECONDARY ACTIVITY:

Sock Puppet Playtime

After the story is finished, have a child open the box and discover the puppets inside. Next, have each child reach in and pull out a sock puppet. Assist the children with putting on their puppets and pretending to be different animals through hand movements and by making animal mannerisms and sounds. (Tip: Include all of animals in the Christmas story, such as a cow, donkey, dove, camel and sheep. This will be a good segue for the next activity.)

THROUGH ACTIVITY:

"The Friendly Beasts" (traditional Christmas song)

Have children stand in a circle with their sock puppets on one hand. Play music and proceed to guide them through a choreographed dance (refer to suggested choreography). Once the dance is completed, collect sock puppets and sit down to review what the children learned.

BEYOND ACTIVITY:

"There Was Much Rejoicing"
(Sophie, Tilly and Phoebe Cryar; Tyler and Travis Franklin)

If time allows, sing "There Was Much Rejoicing." This can be done with or without sock puppets (refer to the next page for words and movements).

SUPPLIES NEEDED:

Faux fireplace
Knowledge of *The Night Before Christmas*
Gift box
Sock puppets for each child in the class
CD player
Recording of "The Friendly Beasts"

ASL: *(for reference, see www.aslpro.com)*

Santa Claus, reindeer, Merry Christmas

MISS FLORETTA SAYS...

This was my opportunity to reconcile Jesus and Santa (if not just for my own benefit), and I did so by making a dance with sock puppets representing all of the animals at the nativity scene. I found the perfect song, "The Friendly Beasts" and from there I had the children follow me with the motions (inspired by Ann Green Gilbert's "Brain Dance") while continuing to "lead with their puppets."

"There Was Much Rejoicing"

(Cryars and Franklins; movements by Erica Oshlick and Laura Wagner)

Bethlehem was buzzing *(both hands shaking up near face; "jazz hands").*
A star was shining bright *(ASL sign for "star").*
There was much rejoicing on that silent night *(wave arms high above head).*
Just how noisy was it *(both arms out to side in a "shrug" position).*

In the stable was a COW . . . moo *(stick head out and say "moo").*
In the stable were some MICE . . . dee dee dee dee *(ASL sign for" mouse").*
In the stable were some SHEEP . . . baaa *(hands by mouth in a calling position).*
In the stable was a donkey . . . hee haw *(swing right arm with fist back and forth).*
With angels from on high. . . . hallelujah *(praying hands).*
A newborn baby cried . . . waaaahhh *(rub eyes with fists as if crying).*

Dancing round the space leading with our sock puppet characters.

"Friendly Beasts" Christmas Program

Dance choreography by Laura Wagner

Distribute sock puppets to children. Stand in a circle facing each other. Begin music.

12-Beat Intro: Stand in circle/adjust puppets

16 Beats: Walk in circle to the right/manipulate puppets

16 Beats, First Verse: Donkey
> walk 4 steps in
> walk 4 steps back
> walk 4 steps in
> walk 4 steps back

16 Beats, Second Verse: Cow
> 8 beats sway right to left/lead with puppet
> 8 beats crouch and walk/turn in low circle as if cow is grazing

16 Beats, Third Verse: Sheep
> 8 beats bounce knees/bounce puppet
> 4 beats tap right toe
> 4 beats tap left toe

16 Beats, Fourth Verse: Dove
> 8 beats flap arms as if flying
> 8 beats flap arms and turn in circle on tip toes

16 Beats, Fifth Verse: Camel
> 8 beats kick out right leg out and in
> 8 beats kick out left leg out and in

16 Beats: Walk in circle to the left/manipulate puppets

Take a bow!

The Brain Dance Breakdown
Handout for Teachers
By Anne Green Gilbert, 2001

Breath: Take 4 or 5 Deep Breaths. Essential for the brain to fully function. The brain uses one-fifth of the body's oxygen.

Tactile: Squeeze, Tap, Slap, Smooth. Leads to sensory integration and promotes appropriate behavior.

Core: Distal "X" and "O." Make a big "X" with the body (as big as possible) then make the body as small as possible by forming an "O" with the body. This "small to big" concept connects interpersonal selves and intrapersonal selves.

Head-Tail. Brings top of head and tail together. This strengthens muscles for sitting, reading and writing.

Upper-Lower: Roll down through spine and swing arms. Move lower half of the body, keeping upper body still. Then keep lower body still and move upper body. This helps the brain isolate body parts to articulate certain tasks.

Body Side, "X" with body: Move with the left side of the body keeping the right side still; then move the right side of the body keeping the left side still. Make a "W" with the arms. Left side to meet right and right to left. Keep eye focused on thumb as it travels. This develops horizontal eye tracking and eye-hand coordination, which helps reading skills.

Cross Lateral: Place elbows to opposite knees in front of and behind body; place hands to opposite feet in front of and behind body. This is a necessary skill for reading and writing. Vertical eye tracking is developed.

Vestibular: Get dizzy! Spin for 15 seconds then spin the other way for 15 seconds. Take deep breaths after spinning to get centered. This stimulates the balance system and helps the body develop balance and coordination.

Getting to know the puppets and pretending they are all different types of animals.

ASL sign for reindeer.

Art + Music = Story!
(Version 1)

 **AIM:** To expose children to fine art and museum etiquette, and teach them a creative way to appreciate visual art by combining art with music and imaginative storytelling. This exercise nurtures an early appreciation for the visual and musical arts.

INTRODUCTION ACTIVITY:

Take a Tour

Prior to class, hang paintings and pictures around the classroom. The pictures should be representative of different emotions and content: a portrait of a man or woman; a landscape, such as a scenic vista of mountains; a still life, such as a picture of fruit or a vase of flowers; an abstract, such as a picture of a blue dot; and realism, such as a lightning storm. These can even be paintings done by the children.

Once the students are settled, pull a paint brush out of your hat. Talk about art and going to the museum. Then take them on an art tour around the room as if you were in a museum. Talk about each piece by asking these questions: What is this a picture of? What is happening in the picture? How does the picture make you feel? Is it a happy or sad picture? What colors did the artist use? When you have completed your tour, seat the children in front of the a projector and screen.

SECONDARY ACTIVITY:

Matching Game! Music with Art

In this matching game, the teacher projects a painting on the screen then plays a sample of music with contrasting emotions. The children must guess what piece of music matches the mood of the painting.

For example, project the image of *A Sunday on La Grande Jatte* by Seurat. Let the kids look at the painting for a moment and discuss together what is happening in the painting. Try to identify if the painting is happy, sad, scary or peaceful. All of the people in the painting are picnicking by the river and the weather seems to be sunny.

Then play for the children the jovial Vivaldi's *Spring* and the gallant Wagner's *The Flying Dutchman*. Ask if the music is happy, sad, scary or peaceful. It will be obvious that Vivaldi matches the painting much better than Wagner. You just made a match! Allow the children to observe the painting with Vivaldi playing in the background and use your imaginations to come up with a story for the painting.

Go through the selected images while playing different clips of music and have the kids match the music. (Be sure to mention the title and artist of each painting, as well as the title and composer of each music selection. Even though the students are not likely nor expected to remember this information, it is good to expose them to idea that there is an artist behind everything they are observing.)

THROUGH ACTIVITY:

Create a Story

Project an image on the screen, such as *Prom Dress* by Norman Rockwell. Ask the children to help come up with a story of what is happening in the picture. Who is she? What is she doing? Why? What do you think will happen? What is the title of our story? Ask children if this is a happy, sad or scary story and play the music clip that applies.

The teacher will then proceed to tell the story of the painting while the music sets the mood in the background. Have the students help tell the story — they will love it! (For help, refer to the Create a Story example on page 35.)

SUPPLIES NEEDED:

Computer	Music clips
Projector	Pre-selected art images
Screen	Art examples to hang on walls
CD player	

ASL: *(for reference, see www.aslpro.com)*

art, music, story

Fine Arts: Create a Story Template

IMAGE:

Prom Dress by Norman Rockwell, 1948.

Begin by asking the children about the emotion of the painting then choose from an index of music to play while you create the story. Have the kids answer the following questions to create a story:

What is her name?
How old is she?
Where is she?
Why did she go there?
What is she doing?
What does she want?
Who owns the dress?
What is their relationship?
Suddenly she hears someone coming. Who is it?
What happens when she is caught?
Where does she go?
How does it end?

The story can be about whatever the students want it to be. Encourage your class to let their imaginations soar and create a whimsical story with an original soundtrack. Here's one example:

Once upon a time, there was a little girl named Anna. She was ten years old and loved to play dress-up. Her older sister, Martha, was soon to be married.

One day, while Martha was busy helping her mother bake cookies, Anna snuck into her sister's room and was tempted to try on Martha's wedding dress. She quietly took the dress out of the closet and held it up to see what it would look like if she were to put it on.

She danced and swirled around the room pretending to be a princess, but just as she was having these thoughts, she heard footsteps coming up the stairs. Anna was terrified! She knew she wasn't allowed to be in her sister's room, let alone playing with her wedding dress, so she quickly put the dress back in the box.

Just as she turned around, Martha entered the room and saw Anna. She started to yell at Anna and ask her what she was doing, but Anna ran past her, down the stairs and out the door as fast as she could. Anna knew she would be in big trouble, but she escaped just in time.

NOTES

_____
_____
_____
_____
_____
_____
_____
_____
_____
_____
_____
_____
_____
_____
_____
_____
_____
_____
_____
_____
_____
_____
_____
_____
_____
_____
_____
_____
_____
_____
_____

Fine Art: Paint Me Colorful!

(Version 2)

 **AIM: The purpose of this lesson is to teach children to identify their emotions, label their feelings with new vocabulary and represent their emotions by color association.**

INTRODUCTION ACTIVITY:

Emotion Cards/Emotion Sculptures

Ask children to stand in a circle. Have each child pull an emotion card out of the hat. Whichever card they pull, have student(s) use their whole body to strike a pose/frozen physical "sculpture" to represent the emotion; for example, happy = a big smile with arms raised up in the air, or sad = a frown with hands wiping the eyes.

After the child gestures, ask them about a time in their life when they felt this way. Proceed around the circle until each child has a chance to pull a card, demonstrate a physical gesture and share a moment. (Emotions can be used more than once, as a wide range of emotions may not be age appropriate for your group.) Emotion examples are: happy, sad, angry, frustrated, peaceful, calm, excited, playful and scared.

SECONDARY ACTIVITY:

Emotions as Colors

Explain to the children that when some artists paint, they use color to express their emotions. Display examples of fine art that exhibit these qualities, for example: *Waterlilies* by Claude Monet for calm; *The Scream* by Edvard Munch for scared; *Dawn After the Wreck* by William Turner for peaceful; *The Ball Players* by Le Douanier Rousseau for playful and happy; *Dr. Paul Gachet* by Vincent Van Gogh for sad. Discuss each painting with the class and determine the emotion of each painting by the colors represented.

Red: Angry
Blue: Calm
White: Peaceful
Yellow: Happy
Orange: Excited
Green: Playful
Black: Scared
Grey: Sad
Brown: Frustrated

THROUGH ACTIVITY:

Song: "If You're Happy and You Know It" (Source: www.kididdles.com)

If you're happy and you know it, clap your hands (clap clap).
If you're happy and you know it, clap your hands (clap clap).
If you're happy and you know it, then your hands will surely show it
If you're happy and you know it, clap your hands (clap clap).

Repeat with: stomp your feet, wiggle your ears, turn in a circle. Ask the students for more examples.

SUPPLIES NEEDED:

Emotion cards
Hat
Examples of paintings

ASL: *(for reference, see www.aslpro.com)*

art, happy, sad, angry, scared, feelings

MISS FLORETTA SAYS... (FOR BOTH VERSIONS 1 AND 2)

Originally, I was concerned that this lesson plan would be too advanced for preschool children. I wasn't exposed to art appreciation until middle school and, even then, it was not that exciting. I only started appreciating art in my late teens and it is something I regret not being exposed to as a small child. Therefore, I made it my goal with this lesson to ignite an early excitement for the visual arts in children as young as three years old.

Even though I was a bit anxious about presenting such "sophisticated" material, I was pleasantly surprised with each new class that walked through the door. The children were excited to take the tour and get to see and talk about the art on the wall. They were also eager to use their imaginations and tell me what they saw in each painting. I realized that kids this young do not have preconceived judgments on this subject matter, therefore, they are not intimidated to dive right in and explore. The exposure to classical music was similar. I found that children love to let the music move them and didn't have any self-consciousness when doing so.

Taking a look at The Storm on the Sea of Galilee *by Rembrandt Van Rijn.*

Fine Arts: Index of Art

PLAYFUL / HAPPY:

A Sunday On La Grande Jatte
Georges Seurat, 1884-86

The Ball Players
Jean-Jacques Rousseau, 1872

Dancing Bears
William Holbrook Beard

SUNRISE / PEACEFUL:

Olive Trees
Vincent Van Gogh, 1889

Sunrise
Claude Monet, 1872

Butterflies
Andy Warhol, 1955

STORM / BRAVERY:

Storm On The Sea Of Galilee
Rembrandt Van Rijn

The Herring Net
Winslow Homer, 1885

Sea Battle
Wassily Kandinsky, 1913

WEDDING / LOVE:

The Wedding Kiss
Consuelo Gamboa

Wedding At The Photographer's
Dagnan-Bouveret, 1878-9

Wedding At Nuremberg
Wilhelm Ritter, 1928

DANCERS / FREEDOM:

The Star, Or Dancer On The Stage
Edgar Degas, 1876-7

Ballerina
Edgar Degas

Blue Dancers
Edgar Degas

DARK / SCARY:

Rouen Cathedral
Claude Monet, 1894

The Actor As The Villain
Katsukawa Shunko (Okubi-e)

Haunted House Cartoon
(artist unknown)

ABSTRACT / CONFUSED:

Grande Baifneuse Au Livre
Pablo Picasso, 1937

The Scream
Edvard Munch, 1893

The Persistence Of Memory
Salvador Dali, 1931

CREATE-A-STORY IMAGE:

Prom Dress
Norman Rockwell, 1949

Fine Arts: Index of Music

PLAYFUL / HAPPY:

Violin Concerto In E, "The Four Seasons (Spring)"
Antonio Vivaldi

SUNRISE / PEACEFUL:

Peer Gynt Suite #1, Op.46
Edvard Greig

STORM / BRAVERY:

The Flying Dutchman Overture
Richard Wagner

WEDDING / LOVE:

Canon In D
Johann Pachelbel

DANCERS / FREEDOM:

Waltz Of The Blue Danube, Op. 314
Johann Strauss, II

DARK / SCARY:

Tocatta And Fugue In D Minor
Johann Sebastian Bach

ABSTRACT / CONFUSED:

Hommage A Soproni
Gyorgy Kurtag and Marta Kurtag

Observing Olive Trees *by Van Gogh, 1889.*

NOTES

Lighting the Way with Shadow Puppets

AIM: The purpose of this lesson is to induce fine motor skills and entertain children through a new medium of storytelling while introducing simple lighting techniques to add effect.

INTRODUCTION ACTIVITY:

Cast the Story: *The Forest Path* by Laura Wagner

Have a light source and a screen set up before class begins. When the children arrive, seat them in an audience formation.

Pull pre-made animal cards out of the hat; the animal choices are rabbit (pink), goose (yellow), dog (blue), elk (green), spider (red) and butterfly (orange). Talk about how each animal is associated with a different color. Follow directions on the provided story worksheet to create a personalized story for your class (the story will be different for each class) then pull a feather out of the hat. Tell the kids that the feather might come in handy later in the story.

SECONDARY ACTIVITY:

Storytelling: *The Forest Path*

Once your characters are decided and you've talked about the feather, turn out the lights and proceed with the shadow story by creating shadow puppets with your hands on the wall or behind the curtain and in front of your light source. When it comes time to solve the riddle, show the feather behind the curtain and see if the students can guess the answer to the riddle by identifying the item's shadow.

THROUGH ACTIVITY:

Casting Shadows

Keep the lights out and quickly review which color represents each animal. Turn on your large light source set up to shine on a blank wall. Show the students that holding up different colored gels in front of the light reflects different colors onto the wall. Demonstrate that if you stand in front of the light, it casts your shadow on the wall.

Now turn on ragtime music ("Maple Leaf Rag" by Scott Joplin, 1899) to set the mood. Choose kids in groups of two or three to stand up in front of the light. Hold up the colored gels in front of the light and have the students pretend to be the animal associated with that color. They can observe their shadows as they move as each of these animals. Change the color gel and instruct the children to match the animal to the color each time; for example, if you hold up the orange gel in front of the light, the kids must pretend they are butterflies and flap their arms to cast a shadow on the wall. Rotate groups until all the children get a chance to be all of the animals.

SUPPLIES NEEDED:

Screen/large white sheet/blank wall
Small light source and large light source
Animal color cards
Feather
Pre-knowledge of a story
Story worksheet
Pre-knowledge of how to make shadow puppets
Blank wall
CD Player
Music: "Maple Leaf Rag" (or any ragtime music)
Colored gels: pink, red, yellow, blue, green, orange
(for reference, see www.shadow-puppets.com)

ASL: *(for reference, see www.aslpro.com)*

light, shadow

MISS FLORETTA SAYS...

The combination of children helping to write the story, watching their story performed in shadow then associating color with movement—all in shadow—is a hit!

Initially, the room I was working in did not have a large blank wall on which to project a light, so I really needed to use my imagination to come up with a way to perform the shadow puppet story so that I can be seen, tell the story and form the shadow animals with my hands all at the same time. (See page 48 for an example of how to make a shadow puppet theater.) It is best to find a spacious empty room where the lights can be turned off with no light contamination from windows or doors. Also, this lesson works best if the room has a large blank wall.

This way, if you don't have a shadow puppet theater, you can use the same light source and wall for both the shadow puppets and for when the kids get up and make their own shadows.

Light set up for the Through Activity: Casting Shadows

The Forest Path Story Template

by Laura Wagner

CHARACTERS: Rabbit   Elk
                    Goose   Spider
                    Dog(s)   Butterfly

(Before you begin, have the children choose a cheerful protagonist, an evil villain with magic words, a nosy character, a friendly character and a clever character from the list above.)

Once upon a time there was a **CHEERFUL**_____(*pick first animal*) named _____(*make up a name!*). He/she absolutely loved to take walks in the woods. He/she would sing to him/herself to pass the time, eat berries, nibble grass and gaze at the puffy white clouds. One day, while _____ was headed home on the forest path, an **EVIL** _____ (*second animal*) jumped out in front of him/her. The _____(*first animal*) was frightened! The _____(*villain*) demanded that he/she answer a riddle if she/he wished to go any farther along the path.

The _____ (*first animal*) had no choice but to agree to answer the riddle, for it was the only path that took her/him home. The villain informed him/her _____ that he/she had only one hour in which to answer the riddle correctly or she/he would be trapped in the forest forever. The villain then cast a spell by saying _____(*evil magic words*), preventing the poor beast from moving from that very spot. The poor beast was trapped there until he/she could work out the riddle. The riddle was: *I fly when I am on and float when I am off. What am I?* Then the evil creature vanished into thin air.

The (*first animal*) thought and thought and thought. Just then, a **FRIENDLY**_____(*third animal*) walked up to him/her.

"Dear friend, why do you look so sad? Surely I can help to cheer you!" The _____ (*first animal*) told him/her the riddle that he/she must solve in order to get home. *I fly when I am on, but float when I am off… What am I?* The new friend thought and thought and thought.

"Maybe it's an airplane?" Just as he uttered the first guess, they heard a cackle of laughter on the breeze and knew that that was not the correct answer. The new friend apologized because it was time to go home and bid him/her a fond farewell. The _____(first animal) sat back under the tree and began to think again.

Just then another animal approached. It was the very **NOSY** _____ (fourth animal). This animal also offered to help out a friend in need and attempted to answer the riddle, *I fly when I am on, but float when I am off… What am I?*

"Maybe it is a mechanical bird," thought the new friend. Again, the leaves rustled and laughter was heard in the distance. Again, the answer was wrong and the new friend must be on his/her way home, for the spell did not hinder any other animal but the _____ (first animal).

By this time, it was getting very dark and out of nowhere stepped up a **CLEVER** _____(fifth animal). This animal was not to be fooled and gave the _____a very helpful clue. The clue seemed to be another riddle. "*I help a bird to sing so sweet but in the springtime, I molt complete. I can be very light and ticklish fun, but when packed together, I weigh a ton.*" Then the clever creature went on his merry way. The _____ was left to contemplate both riddles.

Hmm…*Fly when I am on, float when I am off…Help a bird, light and fun, ticklish, when packed together, weighs a ton.* What on earth could it be? (*Ask the children in audience!*)

A FEATHER! I think you're right! "It's a feather!" and just as _____ (first animal) said the answer, the spell was broken and the path home stretched out before him/her and led the creature back home again.

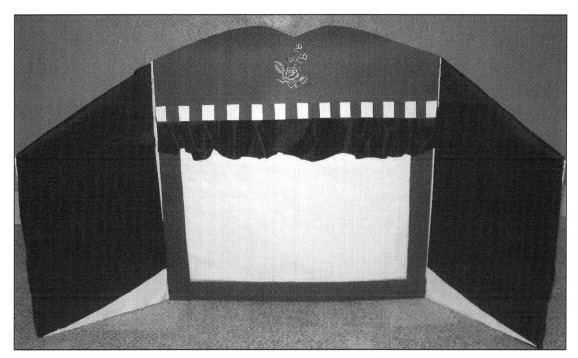

Shadow puppet theatre made from a tri-fold cardboard display, white paper and a little fabric for decoration. Light source is a desk lamp set up behind the theatre.

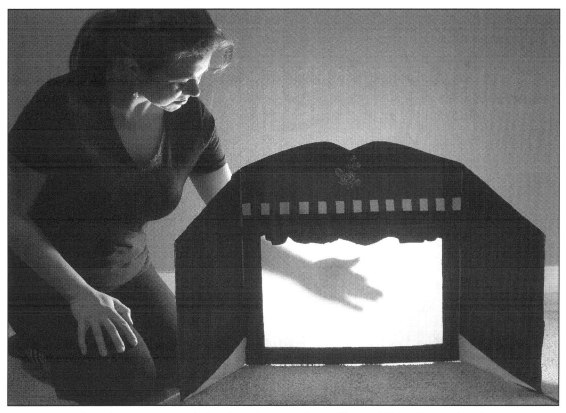

Shadow puppet of the dog during the telling of The Forest Path.

Let's Make Noise!

 **AIM: The purpose of this lesson is to apply sound effects to storytelling to enhance the auditory experience, while incorporating a different medium to broaden sensory perception.**

INTRODUCTION ACTIVITY:

Storytelling: *Jack and the Beanstalk*

Ask the children to sit in a semi-circle and have all sound-making props on display so the children can see them. Demonstrate the noise from each object.

Pull a few beans out of your hat and see if the children can guess what story you will be telling. Recite *Jack and The Beanstalk* using the guide provided on page 51. When the story is complete, be sure to talk over how sound effects can help tell a story and what noises they like the best.

SECONDARY ACTIVITY:

Sound Identification

Have the kids sit in a circle and tell them to close their eyes. Play each instrument in a random order and ask the children if they can associate the sound with each character or moment in the story.

THROUGH ACTIVITY:

Let's Make Noise!

Have the students take turns picking a prop and making noise with it.

BEYOND ACTIVITY:

Sound Identification (continued)

Play several cues from a sound effect CD and have the children guess what sound it is.

SUPPLIES NEEDED:

CD player	Chimes
Sound effects CD	Wood block
Beans	Cowbell
Slide whistle	Noise makers
Tambourine	Drum
Honking horn	Coins in a purse
Maraca	Sandpaper blocks
Kazoo	Triangle

ASL: *(for reference, see www.aslpro.com)*

sound, listen

MISS FLORETTA SAYS...

The set-up for this session is smaller and the kids are sitting much closer than they would be during a presentational story. For this reason, there is a direct flow of energy between the children and the presenter. Having the kids sit up close is not only so they can hear all the sounds better but so they can see the origin of the sound, as well. The students love watching and hearing how sounds help to tell a story. They also take delight in being able to play all of the instruments!

Jack and the Beanstalk
(Ashliman, 1999-2008)

Sound Effects and Story Adaptation by Laura Wagner

Once upon a time, there was a poor mother (jingle purse) who had an only son named Jack (kazoo fanfare). Jack (fanfare) and his mother's (jingle purse) only possession was an old milking cow named Milky White (ring cowbell).

One day, Jack's mother (jingle purse) told Jack (fanfare) to take Milky White (cowbell) to the market to see if he could fetch a price for the old cow so they would have money to buy food. Jack (sad fanfare) was very sad to see his only friend but he did as his mother (jungle purse) said and took the cow (cowbell) to market.

On the way to market, Jack (fanfare) met an old man (shake maraca) who claimed to be a magician. The old man (shake maraca) offered to by the cow (cowbell) in exchange for five magic beans. Jack (fanfare) knew his mother would be upset, but he couldn't resist having five magic beans. The old man (shake maraca) and Milky White (cowbell) walked away and Jack (fanfare) took the magic beans home to his mother (jingle purse).

When (fanfare) returned home, his (jingle purse) was furious! She took the beans, threw them out the window and sent him to bed without any supper. The next morning, (fanfare) woke up early and went to go find the beans before (jingle purse) woke but when he stepped out the door there was an enormous beanstalk in his front yard!

Being curious, (fanfare) started to climb up the beanstalk to see how high it was. He started to climb *(begin low slide whistle)*. He climbed even higher (continue up slide whistle). And even higher (continue even higher with whistle) until he reached the tip-top (complete slide up to highest resonance on slide whistle)! Once he arrived at the top he noticed that there was a huge castle off in the distance and decided that he would go take a closer look.

When he arrived at the enormous door he knocked *(tap on wood block)*. Nobody answered. He knocked again, this time a little louder (knock again with more force); still, no answer. He decided to push the door open very slowly *(turn noisemaker slowly)* until he could squeeze inside. Once inside, he looked all around and saw that the entire castle was covered in gold! *(Ring chimes softly and continue to sound the chimes through the next sentence.)* The floors, the ceiling and even the furniture were completely covered in pure gold! It was truly a sight to behold.

As he walked through the house he came to the kitchen and decided to climb up on the table (quick slide whistle up). On the table he noticed that there was a goose locked in a cage. The goose started honking at him (spastically squeeze bike horn as if talking).

Jack stepped closer to try and understand, but all the goose could say was (spastically squeeze horn a little louder). Jack still couldn't make out what the goose was saying until (one big HONK with horn)! He finally realized that the goose wanted to be set free, but just as he was about to open the cage he heard someone coming (progressively get louder with steady strikes on the drum).

"Fe Fi Fo Fum, I smell the blood of an Englishman!" An enormous giant was storming into the kitchen and Jack (soft fanfare) hurried and jumped (quick pop on the wood block) into a cup to hide.

"Fe Fi Fo Fum," the giant shouted as he sniffed around the kitchen to find the intruder. After what seemed like an eternity, the giant left the kitchen to search elsewhere (fade out drum beats as if giant was walking away). When the coast was clear, Jack jumped back out of the cup (quick pop on the wood block) and hurried to the cage. He slowly opened the door (slow crank of the noise maker) and tucked the goose under his arm (honk!). Oops! Not so tight!

As Jack and the goose headed for the door, the giant returned (play drum beat).

"Fe Fi Fo Fum, I smell the blood of an Englishman!" Jack and the goose ran as fast as they could for the top of the beanstalk and started to slide down (slide whistle down), but the giant was close behind them.

Jack (fanfare) and the goose (honk) made it to the bottom where Jack's mother (jingle purse) was waiting for them. Jack quickly grabbed an ax and started chopping down the beanstalk (quickly rub sandpaper blocks) while his mother made sure the goose was safe. The beanstalk swayed back and forth (jingle tambourine back and forth slowly) until it finally came crashing down with a deafening thud (slam tambourine down on floor). The giant was able to climb back up on the cloud before the beanstalk fell so everyone was safe and he was no longer a threat.

Jack (fanfare) and his mother (jingle purse) gave each other a big hug and while they did they heard the strangest sound (one hit of the finger cymbals) and turned to look at the goose. The goose had laid a golden egg (start playing chimes and continue through the rest of sentence). It was an egg made of solid gold! They were rich and knew they would never want for anything ever again!

So, Jack (kazoo fanfare), his mother (jingle purse) and the goose (honk) lived happily ever after.

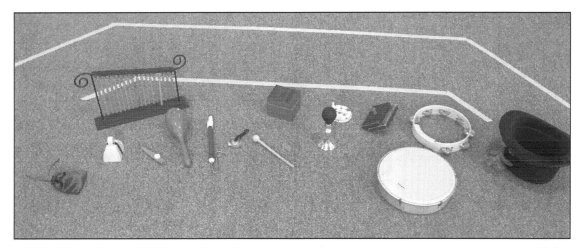

Instrument set-up for Jack and the Beanstalk.

Children engaging their listening skills during the story.

Having fun and sharing a laugh during our listening game.

The Art of Play

NOTES

St. Patrick's Day: Cultural Crosswinds

AIM: The purpose of this lesson is to sharpen mental imagery, hone listening skills, educate on the history of Saint Patrick's Day and expose children to traditional music and dress from The British Isles.

INTRODUCTION ACTIVITY:

Who Do We Celebrate on Saint Patrick's Day?
Saint Patrick, Of Course!

Once the children are seated in audience formation, ask them if they know why we celebrate Saint Patrick's Day. After it has been established that we celebrate the life and story of Saint Patrick, pull a picture of Saint Patrick, a snake and a shamrock out of a hat. Inform the students that snakes and shamrocks are part of the story of Saint Patrick's Day. Proceed to tell the story of Saint Patrick and the history of Saint Patrick's Day (see the story on page 57.)

SECONDARY ACTIVITY:

Bagpipes and Highland Dress

At this point, the instructor will play a short concert for the children. The bagpiper will play for about three to five minutes while the students are engaged in active listening. After this mini-concert is complete, the instructor will explain what he/she is wearing; for example, kilt, gillies, sporran, flashes, Glengarry, and an explanation of what "plaid" is and how important it is to the culture. Children will have a chance to ask questions.

THROUGH ACTIVITY:

Saint Patrick's Day Parade

Have children stand in line while the musician marches them in procession around the room.

BEYOND ACTIVITY:

Create Your Family Tartan

Photocopy the Family Crest activity sheet (page 59) and hand them out to students. Give students a chance to create their own family tartan by drawing their own plaid. Children can also practice writing their last name in the "Clan Name" area of the sheet.

SUPPLIES NEEDED:

World map
Pictures of Saint Patrick, a snake, and a shamrock
Story of Saint Patrick
Bagpiper, bagpipes and Celtic music
Traditional Highland dress
Copies of Family Crest activity sheet
Crayons

ASL: *(for reference, see www.aslpro.com)*

green

MISS FLORETTA SAYS...

This program teaches both music and world culture. I dress in my Scottish regalia and tell the story of Saint Patrick, then I describe my outfit and play the Scottish small-pipes for them. (The highland bagpipes would be much too loud for little ears.) Then we march in our own parade.

If you don't have access to a bagpiper, you can substitute with a video of bagpiping or a recording of Celtic music. You can even play Irish tunes on different instruments if you or someone you know plays these instruments.

The story of Saint Patrick is universal (everyone is Irish on Saint Patrick's Day!). It is important enough to transcend religious boundaries and can be understood and appreciated at any age.

The Story of Saint Patrick

A Children's Adaptation by Laura Wagner

Once upon a time, a long time ago in the country of Scotland, there was a young lad named Patrick. Patrick's family was very, very rich. They lived in a stone castle, slept on the softest beds, ate the most delicious meals and dressed in the finest clothes. It might be smart to say that Patrick never wanted for anything.

But Patrick was rich in a different way, too. Every day while growing up, Patrick would go with his friends to play in the green meadows of the Scottish countryside. There were big rocks on which to climb, fields in which to run and beaches on which to play. Patrick loved his country and he prayed to God every day, thanking him for his wonderful land and all of his many, many gifts.

One day when Patrick was sixteen years old, an angry band of pirates sailed up to shore and captured him. He was scared, confused and angry. He didn't know what was going to happen next and was very frightened. To calm down and gain control over all his feelings, he took deep breaths and began thinking positive thoughts. He thought of happy times with his family, how God has never failed him before, and how thankful he was to be alive.

The wicked pirates took him to another country known as Ireland, and made him live and work there as a shepherd. All of a sudden, Patrick found himself in a strange new land, far away from the family that loved him.

Though he worked hard every day for a very mean sheep owner, Patrick never stopped praying to God. One day while Patrick was tending the sheep in the fields, he decided to lie down and gaze up at the puffy white clouds. He breathed in and out slowly and let his imagination soar. Suddenly he started having visions. In one breath, he saw a cloud that looked like a shamrock and when he breathed again, he saw another cloud that looked like a snake. When he took one last deep breath, he saw a puffy cloud that looked just like a ship sailing on the ocean. Patrick believed that the shapes in the clouds were a sign from God to go to the beach.

Patrick walked a long way to the shore and, lo and behold, he saw the very same ship that appeared to him in the sky! He snuck onto the ship and sailed far away from the pirates that had captured him years before. He breathed a sigh of relief as the ship got farther away.

Patrick knew that God had showed him the way to escape from the pirates. He also knew that if he calmed himself, breathed deeply and used his imagination, that he could hear God's advice much more clearly.

Years later, when Patrick became a man, he decided to devote his life to God by becoming a priest. He spent his days spreading God's message of love and peace but there was something that continued to trouble Patrick. He remembered that fateful day when he saw the visions. There were two other images up in the sky: a shamrock and a snake. Patrick believed the shamrock was a sign to go back to Ireland and teach the Irish people about God's message of love and peace. He described the mystery of God by using the image of a shamrock. The three leaves represent the Father, the Son and the Holy Spirit in one clover. Patrick also proved the power of this message by shooing away all the snakes on Ireland. To this day you will not find a single snake on the island of Ireland!

Patrick is the patron saint of Ireland, and every year we celebrate his story and remember his message of peace, love and thankfulness for our many, many gifts.

Family Crest

Clan Name: _____

Their first introduction to Scottish small-pipes.

Voice Acting: Sing a Rainbow

AIM: The purpose of this lesson is to teach children that their voices are special, that no two people sound exactly alike and that we can use our unique voices to express our individuality. It makes children aware that voices are like different colors of the rainbow and that our voices can be a tool for making art.

INTRODUCTION ACTIVITY:

Video Story: *I Can Find God* by Laura Wagner

Show the video story of the book *I Can Find God (or any story/video that would be appropriate)*. In addition to following the story and retaining its message, have children focus on the voice of the narrator. See if they can guess who is speaking (if possible, have the teacher record their voice narrating the story). Ask them how they know that it's the teacher's voice. The answer is because it sounds like the teacher! They will be able to tell that it's my voice because my voice doesn't sound like anyone else's, just as their voices sound exactly like them! Explain that each voice is unique and is just like a color of the rainbow.

SECONDARY ACTIVITY:

Voice Recordings

Have three students at a time step up on stage. Record the children introducing themselves. Tell them to speak this into the audio recorder: "Hello, my name is _____ and my favorite color is _____." Record all three children at the same time. After they are finished speaking into the recorder, play back the voices to the class and see if they can guess which voice belongs to which child. Continue until all the children have had a chance to record their voices and hear them played back.

THROUGH ACTIVITY:

Song: "I Can Sing a Rainbow" (Source: www.kids.neih.nih.gov)

While the children are sitting, teach them the signs for the colors red, yellow, pink, green, purple, orange, blue and rainbow. Have the children stand in a line; starting at one end, ask each child to repeat with confidence: "Hello, my name is _____."

Determine what "color" you think their voice sounds like and pull a colored scarf out of a hat. Go down the line until each child states their name and is given a colored scarf. Once each child has a scarf, remain standing and begin to sing and sign this song:

Red and yellow and pink and green.
Purple and orange and blue.
I can sing a rainbow (sweep scarf overhead, as in the sign for "rainbow")
Sing a rainbow (sweep scarf overhead the other way)
Sing a rainbow, too. (sweep one more time)

SUPPLIES NEEDED:

Video of *I Can Find God* by Laura Wagner (www.lauralynnewagner.com)
Copy of the book *I Can Find God*
TV with DVD player
Audio recorder and speakers
Colored scarves

ASL: *(for reference, see www.aslpro.com)*

rainbow, red, yellow, pink, green, purple, orange, blue, sing

MISS FLORETTA SAYS...

This lesson is a great opportunity for children to literally "find their voice." Most preschool-aged children have never heard a recording of their own voice and it is such a thrill to watch each child react to hearing their voice played back to them. I was particularly excited when a young girl who has selective mutism spoke in front of the class! Needless to say, her teachers were ecstatic and I think she was, too! This lesson is an attempt to target different learning styles by incorporating visual, kinesthetic, spiritual and musical intelligences.

Waving our colorful scarves and making a rainbow!

Teaching ASL signs to the "I Can Sing a Rainbow" song.

Three kids up on stage speaking into a digital recorder.

NOTES

_____
_____
_____
_____
_____
_____
_____
_____
_____
_____
_____
_____
_____

Do You Have Something to Say?

AIM: The purpose of this lesson is to heighten children's self-esteem, to find their voices and empower them to believe that they can make a difference in the betterment of the world.

INTRODUCTION ACTIVITY:

Storytelling: *Ruby Mae Has Something To Say* by David Small

Have students sit in an audience formation or semi-circle while the teacher presents the story. (This story would not be complete without a large metal colander with lots of trinkets hanging off of it!) After the story, briefly discuss its message and meaning.

SECONDARY ACTIVITY:

Hat Box

Play a fun bit of background music to set a festive mood. Have the children choose a hat from a box of different hats. Be sure to tell them in advance that the hat they choose is the hat they will wear, unless another student is willing to swap. Give them a minute or two to look at themselves in the mirror and react to what they see.

THROUGH ACTIVITY:

Public Speaking

Set up a small pedestal or podium, complete with a microphone, on which the students can step up one at a time (encourage them to keep their hats on) and have the chance to tell a story. Feel free to give them prompts, such as "tell me about your trip to the beach" or "tell me about your favorite stuffed animal." Use your instincts to prompt them to think of a story. Not all children will want to get up and speak, and that is okay. Some children will want to speak more than once. Again, it is up to the teacher to monitor and guide the students so that everyone who wants to speak gets a chance to use their voice and share a story.

BEYOND ACTIVITY:

Social Action

If you are interested in expanding this activity into a longer session or an alternate session, try challenging the kids into more public speaking. Ask the children to step up to the podium to announce what they would do to make the world a better place. Have an assistant record answers on the provided worksheet (page 68) and take a picture of each student wearing their fabulous hat. Once the pictures are developed, paste them to their sheets and display with pride!

SUPPLIES NEEDED:

Knowledge of the story *Ruby Mae Has Something To Say*
Colander with lots of trinkets hanging off of it
Box of different hats
Mirror
Small platform
A pretend microphone (or real one, if desired)
Copies of worksheet
Pens or markers
Glue or tape
Camera
CD player and selections of music

ASL: *(for reference, see www.aslpro.com)*

president, confidence, story

MISS FLORETTA SAYS...

Public speaking can be scary at any age. This program is designed to let children stand in the spotlight and have a chance to talk. We spend so much time trying to quiet children down that there isn't much opportunity for their voices to be heard.

Ruby Mae Has Something to Say by David Small is the perfect blend of all the elements in this program. It introduces public speaking, letting your voice be heard, wearing hats and how much dramatic fun this can be. It also promotes global peace and tranquility.

When the children are given an opportunity to try on different hats and pick one to wear as they told their story, it gives them a sense that they are dressing up "in character"; this eases a lot of the pressure of standing up in front of everyone. Of course, the students should never be forced to stand up and tell a story but it is always pleasantly surprising to see the ones who choose to do it!

 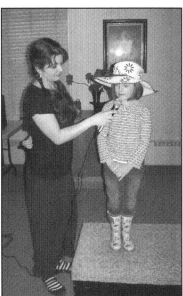 

These children definitely have something to say!

I Can Make a Difference!

[place photo here]

Name: _____

What I would do to change the world and make it a better place:

_____

_____

_____

_____

_____

"Thank You!"

It was so good to be here together!

Thanks for spending time with me. I hope that the lessons we shared spark the creativity and love of learning that's within all of us!

Until we meet again,

Miss Floretta

ASL sign for thunderous applause!

Acknowledgements

For the help in bringing this book into being, I would like to heartily thank the following people:

Bonnie Getkin and Robin Macon for placing their trust in me and inspiring the idea of the CAP Program in the first place.

The teachers and staff of Ingomar Child Enrichment Center for their cooperation and willingness to play along with their school children.

The faculty of the University of Montana's Drama/Dance Department and Creative Pulse Program for their professional advice and guidance.

Mary Morgan-Smith from Northland Public Library who daily advocates the importance of reading and storytelling and who first inspired me to start telling stories.

Gina Mazza and Holly Rosborough for their expertise and creativity in making this book truly a collaborative effort.

Karen "Mrs. C" Cordaro, my lifelong mentor, for teaching me that through creativity and imagination all things are possible.

My husband, Chris, my son, Ethan and my dear parents and family for being a constant source of love, inspiration and support.

Sister Floretta Fuchs of the Sisters of Saint Francis, my heavenly namesake.

Bibliography

"Aiken Drum." Traditional Scottish Carol. www.kididdles.com

"Apples and Bananas." www.kididdles.com

Ashliman, D.L., editor. *Three Little Pigs and Other Folktales.* 1999-2008.

Commedia Del'Arte. www.theatrehistory.com

"First Thanksgiving: Poem Style." www.tooter4kids.com

Gardner, Howard. *Frames of Mind: The Theory of Multiple Intelligences.* New York: Basic Books, 1983.

Green Gilbert, Anne. *The Brain Dance.* www.creativedance.org, 2000.

"If You're Happy and You Know It." www.kididdles.com

Joplin, Scott. "Maple Leaf Rag," 1899.

Lang, Andrew. *Jack and the Beanstalk.* London: Longmans, Green and Co., 1895.

"Legend of the Snake with the Big Feet." www.firstpeople.us

Madacy Entertainment. *Sixty Christmas Carols for Kids.* Quebec: 2005.

Matsutani, Miyoko. *Momotaro, The Peach Boy.* New York.

Moore, Clement C. *The Night Before Christmas.* www.christmas-tree.com

Mulvihill, Margaret. *The Treasury of Saints and Martyrs.* New York: Viking, 1999.

Murray, Carol Garboden. *Simple Signing With Young Children.* Beltsville: Gryphon House, 2007.

"Rain Dance." www.teacherlink.edu

"Skip to My Lou." www.kididdles.com

"Sing a Rainbow." www.kids.nieh.nih.gov

Small, David. *Ruby Mae Has Something to Say.* Crown, 1992.

"There Was Much Rejoicing." Recorded by Sophie, Tilly and Phoebe Cryar, and Tyler and Travis Franklin from the album *Go Tell It On the Mountain: The Music of Christmas.*

Wagner, Laura. *I Can Find God.* Lulu Press, 2009.

Photography:

Jessica Franks, Becky Smith, Sandy Sholze, Yvonne Dominick, Laura Wagner

Made in the USA
Charleston, SC
30 January 2012